Island Ave Elementary Sc'

37602150000285

SPORTS' GREATEST RIVALRIES

YANKEES VS. RED SOX

Parker Holmes

PowerKiDS press.

New York

Published in 2014 by The Rosen Publishing Group, Inc.
29 East 21st Street, New York, NY 10010

First Edition

Editor: Julie Zerbib
Book Design: Dean Galiano

Photo Credits: (front, top) Cover Sporting News/Getty Images, (front, bottom) Jim McIsaac/Getty Images, (back, bottom) Diamond Images/Getty Images, (back, top) Al Bello/Getty images, Michael Heiman/Getty Images, Ezra Shaw/Getty Images, Transcendental Graphics/Getty Images; p. 2-3 (background image) Jared Wickerham/Getty Images; p. 5 Transcendental Graphics/Getty Images; p. 6 (right) MLB Photos/Getty Images, (left) Sports Studio Photo/Getty Images; p. 7 Michael Heiman/Getty Images; p. 9 Matthew Stockman/Getty Images, (inset) Transcendental Graphics/Getty Images; p. 11 Topical Press Agency/Getty Images; p. 12 (left) Rick Stewart/Getty Images, (right) Dick Raphael/Sports Illustrated/Getty Images; p. 13 Dick Raphael/Sports Illustrated/Getty Images; p. 15 Al Bello/Getty Images; p. 17 Ezra Shaw/Getty Images; p. 18 (left) Sporting News/Getty Images, (right) Transcendental Graphics/Getty Images; p. 19 Jim Rogash/Getty Images.

Library of Congress Cataloging-in-Publication Data

Holmes, Parker.
 Yankees vs. Red Sox / by Parker Holmes. -- First edition.
     pages cm. -- (Sports' greatest rivalries)
 Includes index.
 ISBN 978-1-4777-2777-5 (library binding) -- ISBN 978-1-4777-2778-2 (pbk.) -- ISBN 978-1-4777-2779-9 (6-pack)
 1. New York Yankees (Baseball team)--History--Juvenile literature. 2. Boston Red Sox (Baseball team)--History--Juvenile literature. 3. Sports rivalries--United States--Juvenile literature. I. Title.
 GV875.N4H65 2014
 796.357'640974--dc23
                              2013010305

Manufactured in the United States of America

CPSIA Compliance Information: Batch #W13PK5: For Further Information contact Rosen Publishing, New York, New York at 1-800-237-9932

CONTENTS

Baseball's Best Rivalry 4

The Bronx Bombers 6

Red Sox Nation 8

Curse of the Bambino 10

Bucky Dent's Homer 12

The Eleventh Inning Shot... 14

The Comeback 16

The Game Goes On.. 18

Yankees vs. Red Sox Timeline 20

Yankees-Red Sox Head-to-Head 22

Glossary 23

Index 24

Websites.. 24

BASEBALL'S BEST RIVALRY

The Yankees versus the Red Sox! It's the most famous **rivalry** in baseball history. In fact, it may be the most famous rivalry in all of American sports. The New York Yankees and the Boston Red Sox have been playing each other for more than a hundred years, and the rivalry today is as strong as ever.

Boston and New York have played many great games over the years. Both teams are in the American League. That means they compete for the chance to play in the World Series against the champion of the National League. The Yankees have stopped the Red Sox from getting to the World Series many times. This is a big reason why the rivalry is so **intense**.

Even though the Yankees have come out on top more often than the Red Sox, the competition is always exciting. These two teams love to beat each other more than they do any other team in the league.

Red Sox outfielder Ted Williams (left) and Yankee Babe Ruth hold a bat before a game in 1939. Williams and Ruth were two of the best hitters of all time.

THE BRONX BOMBERS

The Yankees are the most **successful** team in Major League Baseball history. They have won 27 World Series. That's more than twice as many as any other team! The Yankees won their first World Series in 1923. That was also the first year the team played in its new stadium in the Bronx in New York City.

Yankee Lou Gehrig was a strong hitter and almost never missed a game. He was nicknamed "The Iron Horse." Shown at right is Yankees power hitter Mickey Mantle.

Yankees Alex Rodriguez (#13) and Derek Jeter celebrate after Rodriguez hits his 600th career home run.

In 2009, the Yankees moved to a bigger stadium that cost around $1.5 billion. It's one of the most expensive sports stadiums in the world. When the Yankees play at home, they wear their famous **pinstriped** home uniforms.

Many of the best athletes in baseball have played on the Yankees **roster**. How many Yankees superstars can you name? Babe Ruth, Lou Gehrig, Joe DiMaggio, Yogi Berra, Mickey Mantle, and Derek Jeter are just a few of them.

RED SOX NATION

Fans of the Boston Red Sox love to cheer for their team. They are some of the most **loyal** sports fans in the country. The Red Sox are located in Boston, Massachusetts, and the team has an incredible history. Boston won the very first World Series, way back in 1903.

Many great athletes have played for the Red Sox. Cy Young, Ted Williams, Carl Yastrzemski, Pedro Martinez, and David Ortiz are just a few of the outstanding players that Boston fans have cheered for over the years.

Boston plays in Fenway Park, the oldest major league stadium in the country. The Red Sox have played there since 1912. Do you know what the left-field wall of Fenway is called? It's known as the Green Monster, and it's the highest outfield wall in Major League Baseball.

EMC LEVEL

Pedro Martinez was one of Boston's best pitchers. In 1999, he struck out 17 Yankees in one game. (inset) Pitcher Cy Young played on the first Boston team in 1901.

CURSE OF THE BAMBINO

Before 1920, the Red Sox had enjoyed more success than their New York rivals. Boston had won five World Series, and the Yankees hadn't won any. But then, suddenly, everything changed. The Red Sox owner sold the team's best player, Babe Ruth, to the Yankees. In New York, Ruth became the most famous player in the sport. He broke home run records and helped the Yankees win four World Series.

After Ruth joined them, the Yankees became the greatest team in baseball. Meanwhile, the Red Sox went 86 years before they won another World Series. Some Red Sox fans wondered if they went so long without a championship because the team let Ruth go. How big a mistake was it to sell Ruth to New York? Many Red Sox fans felt their team was **cursed** for sending Ruth to the Yankees. Since Ruth's nickname was "the **Bambino**," some people called Boston's bad **fortune** the "Curse of the Bambino."

Red Sox fans wish Babe Ruth hadn't been sold to the Yankees. What do you think would have happened if Ruth had stayed in Boston?

BUCKY DENT'S HOMER

The Yankees and Red Sox have played many close games over the years. One **memorable** matchup took place at the end of the 1978 season. Boston and New York were tied for first place in their **division**. The current playoff system hadn't started yet, so the teams played a single game to decide the winner of the American League East.

The Green Monster in Boston is the highest outfield wall in the league. Yankee Bucky Dent (right) hits a homer over the Green Monster to help win a 1978 game.

Bucky Dent celebrates with his Yankees teammates after hitting a home run. His home run was surprising because Dent wasn't known for his power hitting.

After six innings, things were looking good for Boston. The Red Sox led, 2–0. Then in the seventh, with two outs and two men on base, Yankees shortstop Bucky Dent stepped up to bat. Dent wasn't a power hitter. He had hit only four home runs all season. But guess what? He slapped a homer over the Green Monster and put New York ahead, 3–2. The Yankees won the game and went on to win the World Series.

THE ELEVENTH INNING SHOT

Boston and New York had another tense showdown in 2003. They met in the American League Championship Series, and it turned into a hard-fought battle. They each had won three games, so it came down to a final game to decide who would go to the World Series.

During that last game, Boston pitcher Pedro Martinez went up against Yankees pitcher Roger Clemens. The Red Sox jumped ahead and led, 4–2, after the seventh inning. But the Yankees fought back to tie it up and send the game to extra innings. In the eleventh inning, Yankee Aaron Boone came to bat. He faced **knuckleball** pitcher Tim Wakefield. On the first pitch, Boone hit a ball— whack!—right out of the park to win the game. Red Sox fans would have to wait another year to get **revenge**.

Yankee Aaron Boone hits a winning home run against the Red Sox. Boone became the hero of the 2003 playoffs. His homer won the series for New York.

THE COMEBACK

The Red Sox got another chance to play the Yankees for the American League championship in 2004. It didn't start well for Boston. The Yankees won the first three games. The teams were playing a best-of-seven series. The first team to win four games wins the series. Boston had to win four straight times to win the championship. No team in history had ever come back from that far behind. Most people doubted that the Red Sox could pull it off.

The fourth game was a classic. It went to 12 innings before Red Sox hitter David Ortiz came to the rescue. He knocked a two-run homer to win the game. The Red Sox were still alive. In the next game, Ortiz saved the team again. He drove in the winning run in the 14th inning. Now the Red Sox needed to win two more games. Could they do it? Yes! The Red Sox beat the Yankees. Boston then went on to win the World Series against the St. Louis Cardinals. For the first time in 86 years, the Red Sox were the champions of baseball!

Slugger David Ortiz saves the Red Sox after hitting a winning home run. His homer kept the Red Sox alive during the 2004 playoffs against the Yankees.

THE GAME GOES ON

The Red Sox and Yankees have a long and exciting history. They've played each other more than 2,000 times, with the Yankees winning a little more than half of the matchups. During those games, fans have been treated to so many great moments. There were many times when fans got to watch Babe Ruth blast home runs. There was the summer of 1941,

Yankee Joe DiMaggio (left) and Ted Williams of Boston meet before a game. They thrilled fans with their batting, especially during 1948. Babe Ruth is shown at right.

Red Sox and Yankees fans pose before a game. Fans have cheered for these two teams for more than 100 years. Which team do you cheer for?

when fans were on the edge of their seats watching the record-breaking batting of Joe DiMaggio and Ted Williams. There were all the close division **pennant** races. There were all the times when it took extra-inning **heroics** to win a game. The list of great moments in this rivalry is long, and it will keep getting longer. Yankees and Red Sox fans can't wait to see what happens next!

YANKEES VS. RED SOX TIMELINE

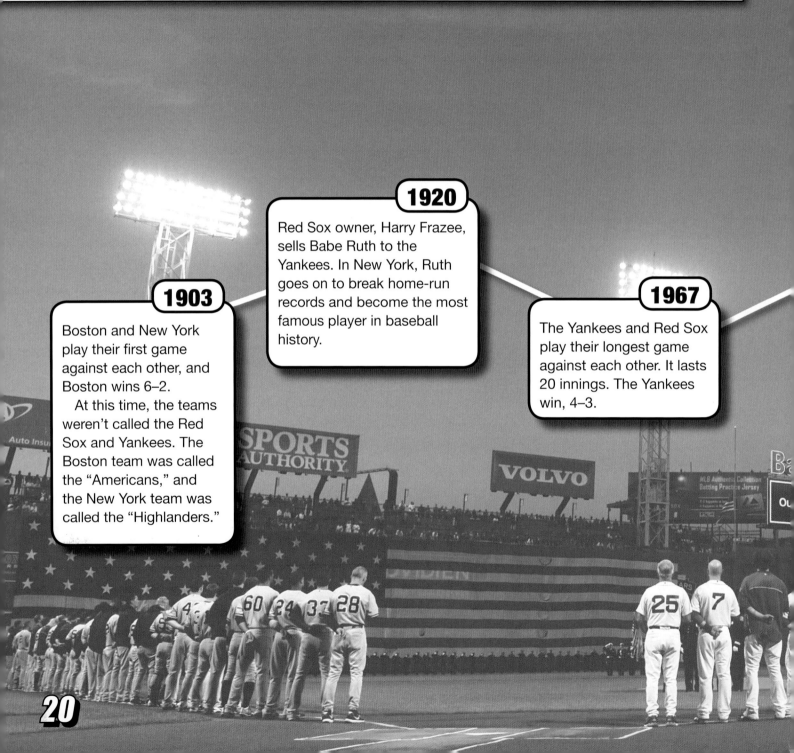

1920

Red Sox owner, Harry Frazee, sells Babe Ruth to the Yankees. In New York, Ruth goes on to break home-run records and become the most famous player in baseball history.

1903

Boston and New York play their first game against each other, and Boston wins 6–2.

At this time, the teams weren't called the Red Sox and Yankees. The Boston team was called the "Americans," and the New York team was called the "Highlanders."

1967

The Yankees and Red Sox play their longest game against each other. It lasts 20 innings. The Yankees win, 4–3.

1976

A fight breaks out among players at a Red Sox-Yankees game. Boston pitcher Bill Lee hurts his shoulder in the fight. It takes months for Lee to recover.

1978

During a tiebreaker game to decide the American League East championship, Yankee Bucky Dent hits a home run and New York beats Boston. The Yankees go on to win the World Series.

1999

Red Sox pitcher Pedro Martinez strikes out 17 Yankees in one game. No pitcher has ever struck out that many Yankees in a single game.

2000

New York beats Boston, 22–1, at Fenway Park. It's the most lopsided home-field loss in Red Sox history.

2004

The Red Sox beat the Yankees in the playoffs and go on to win their first World Series since 1918.

YANKEES-RED SOX HEAD-TO-HEAD

	Yankees	Red Sox
Team Location	Bronx, New York	Boston, Massachusetts
Date Founded	1903	1901
Stadium Capacity	50, 287	37, 493
World Series Championships	27	7
American League Pennants	40	12
Team Colors	Dark Blue, White, and Gray	Red, White, and Dark Blue
Hall of Fame Players*	34	32
Most Valuable Player Awards**	20	10

*Played at least part of their careers with the Yankees or Red Sox.

**The American League selects one player a year as Most Valuable Player. Five Yankees and one Red Sox player have won it more than once.

GLOSSARY

BAMBINO (BAM-bee-noh) The Italian word for "baby."

CURSED (KURSD) When bad things happen to someone.

DIVISION (dih-VIH-zhun) A separate group.

FORTUNE (FOR-chun) The way things turn out.

HEROICS (hih-ROH-iks) When someone does something great.

INTENSE (in-TENTS) Done with lots of energy and feelings.

KNUCKLEBALL (NUH-kel-bahl) A pitch that moves in unusual ways.

LOYAL (LOY-ul) Sticking with someone; being faithful.

MEMORABLE (MEM-ruh-bel) Able to be remembered easily.

PENNANT (PEH-nunt) A type of championship awarded to the winners of the regular season.

PINSTRIPED (PIN-strypd) Clothing that has thin lines running up and down.

REVENGE (rih-VENJ) Getting even with someone.

RIVALRY (RY-vul-ree) Competition between teams that play each other a lot and feel strongly about winning.

ROSTER (ROS-tur) The players who make up a team.

SUCCESSFUL (suk-SES-ful) Being good at something.

INDEX

A
American League, 4, 12, 14, 16, 21

B
Berra, Yogi, 7
Boone, Aaron, 14, 15

C
Clemens, Roger, 14

D
Dent, Bucky, 12, 13
DiMaggio, Joe, 7, 18, 19

F
Fenway Park, 8, 21

G
Gehrig, Lou, 6, 7
Green Monster, 8, 12

J
Jeter, Derek, 7

M
Mantle, Mickey, 6, 7
Martinez, Pedro, 8, 9, 14, 21

N
National League, 4

O
Ortiz, David, 8, 16, 17

P
pennant, 19

R
Rodriguez, Alex, 7
Ruth, Babe, 5, 7, 10, 11, 18, 20

W
Wakefield, Tim, 14
Williams, Ted, 5, 8, 18, 19
World Series, 4, 8, 10, 13, 14, 16, 21

Y
Yastrzemski, Carl, 8
Young, Cy, 8, 9

WEBSITES

Due to the changing nature of Internet links, PowerKids Press has developed an online list of websites related to the subject of this book. This site is updated regularly. Please use this link to access the list:
www.powerkidslinks.com/cfgr/yankssox/